THE ART OF FLIPPING BRICKS

DOUGLAS PARSON JR.
WITH CLARENCE KD MCNAIR

For information regarding special discounts for bulk purchases, please contact the publisher: LaBoo Publishing Enterprise, LLC

staff@laboopublishing.com
www.laboopublishing.com

TABLE OF CONTENTS

DEDICATION

To my mother Patricia Parson, I want to thank you for all the sacrifices you made for me as a child. All of the great conversations we have now, and many more to come. I thank God that you're my mother. To my sons Dasmond, Dajon (RIP), Douglas III, Drezyn, and Dealo, I pray that you too find your passion and purpose in life. May seeing my hard work, dedication, and tireless hours be an inspiration for you. Each one of you has taught me life lessons in one way or another. My grandmother (Bellina Rose) and grandfather (George Rose), who passed away, may your spirit and bond help me here on Earth. How I wish you two would have lived to see my great accomplishments. My Rose family, thank you for your prayers and inspiration over the years and into my adulthood. Last but not least, to my wife, Dr. Atiya Parson, you saw my vision, my dreams, accepted my flaws, and every step of the way loved me unconditionally. I say this and mean it with every part of me. You are truly my angel, and I thank God for having you in my life.

ACKNOWLEDGMENTS

Thank you…

- God first

- My wife Dr. Atiya Parson who always believed in me and kept me going through all the ups and downs on the way up. She is my angel

- My kids and my mother Pistol Pat

- Elizabeth Johnson, who got me in the real estate business

- Rod Williams, who gave me a spark when I was burnt out on real estate

- Kevin "Coach K" Lee, Young Joc, Pre Madonna, Safaree Samuels, and Twin (#noigtwin). They all put me in position to work with some of the biggest celebrities in the country

- Last but not least, Clarence KD McNair for believing in me and pushing me toward greatness

Thank you to the hidden gems...

I would like to give special acknowledgments to a few people who took the time to contribute and add their wealth of knowledge to my book. These people have gems to drop that have taken their level of the real estate game to a whole different level.

Thank you to Virgil Gordon who offered his expertise on securing an unconventional type of loan, Tia Williams, the credit repair genius, Howard Smithsonertise for offering assistance and guidance in reference to hard money loans, Kendra Robinson added her flare on finding and using the right real estate attorney, Tiffany Veney, CEO of Madison Street Design and Build Group, Julie small, CEO Julie Dream Realty, McNair Books family and LaBoo Publishing Enterprise, I will be forever grateful for their time and expertise.

FOREWORD

I heard about Doug Parson in the early '90s, and everything that I heard about him was real! When I finally met him, everything that I heard, and saw was true. He's a true hustler and was really smooth with it. The city of Indianapolis where we come from, there weren't too many opportunities for a young Black man. You either went to work in a blue-collar factory job, or you were subjected to the streets for income. Doug had vision, passion, and drive. And I must say he beat the streets, which is very hard to do. He went from flipping bricks to literally flipping bricks. Different product but same hustle. I can say Doug is one of my brothers, because we share the same story. We both left Indianapolis around the same time with a plan to change the reality that we faced. I chose music, and Doug chose real estate. I watched him really hustle his products into the operation you see today. Built from the ground up. The beautiful thing is he found and sold me my dream house. I can attest that in this book you will be taught some gems that will stick with you. I'm proud of my brother for focusing and telling His-Story!

– Kevin "Coach K" Lee

TESTIMONIALS

I reached out to Doug about a commercial space needed to build an entertainment complex with enough space to suit all of our needs. Before we exited the phone call Doug told me to check my email. Wouldn't you know it, he'd already sent me a load of listings that fit my criteria to shop through. After a few searches, my partner and I (ATL Jacob) decided to bid on a building we deemed perfect for our venture. Doug was a joy to work with from the initial phone call all the way to the closing table! Even thereafter, he continues to check and see how things are going. I'll definitely hire Doug for ALL of my real estate needs.

**– Jacob and Iren Golder,
Multi-Platinum Producer ATL**

Doug started off as our realtor and ended up becoming a great friend! He was very precise with finding us what we needed in our home, and that is a true definition of a hustler! At times we wanted to give up on looking for a home, but he was persistent with sending us new homes to view!

With that being said, I already know his book is going to be AMAZING and I can't wait to get my signed copy! If you can flip bricks, you can definitely flip homes or businesses! I'm in sales so I know what it is and I definitely can relate! It literally took us 45 days to find, get approved and close on our multimillion-dollar dream home with Doug and we definitely appreciate him for that!

– Sierra Gates and Eric Whitehead

Working with Doug was a pleasure and the best 1st time home buyer experience ever! He helped me get my dream home and never gave up! We looked for over a year and he made it happen and kept his word! Doug the plug for president 🙏

– Safaree Samuels

Doug and I met in 2009 at a recording studio in Atlanta. At the time I was beginning my career as an artist manager overseeing the release of an upcoming mixtape *Infatuated with Money* by artist LT. My management career was short lived, but it was during that time when Doug and I built a good relationship.

Since Doug had a good relationship with the record label and studio owner, I would often vent to him about my frustrations with the lack of momentum with my current role. I vividly recall Doug telling me he thought I would be great in real estate, and I should seriously consider it.

That conversation really stuck with me because I honestly had no idea Doug was in real estate lol. I figured he was in the music business or drug business due to his urban attire and vehicle of choice. Once I found out he was a realtor my life changed forever. For the first time I realized I could switch gears in my career, do something totally left field but still maintain my cool by dressing like Doug lol.

In 2010 I obtained my real estate license under the mentorship of Doug and never looked back. I've since built a seven-figure real estate sales team and recognized as the #1 Black owned real estate team in Atlanta.

Doug has been the most influential person on my journey in real estate and I couldn't have achieved this level of success without his guidance.

– Rod Williams, CEO Of The Williams Team Keller Williams #1 Black Owned Real Estate Team in Atlanta

I'm very pleased with this read...from the concept to the content!!! Doug is a personal friend of mine and also my realtor. Time and time again, he's pulled off magic and miracles with his knowledge of the business and the savviness of his approach to the business. I hope you find wisdom and the answers you've been looking for in this book.

– **Yung Joc**

Doug is not just a realtor, he's a genuine people connector. Over the last decade, whether it's been finding me a real estate deal or setting up a game-changing meeting for me, one thing's for sure: Doug is the "Plug".

– **Smoot Films**

INTRODUCTION

There's an art to everything, even in hustling. Just like a decision after a few life experiences, it can become a special skill. Remember you're one decision away from your goals, your dreams, your future, and your family legacy. I'm sure when you picked this book up maybe you expected to get right to the money, aka the bag. However, before we can get to the money and get to the bag I felt that it was very important to look at this thing called investment from another perspective. The fact that you picked up this book is a sign that something inside of you knows that it's time to change, or something inside you knows that there's no other way. When you think about generational wealth, most people think investments. Most people think about money. It's why most people do what they do, to make money. I'm hoping that after reading this book your outlook on life will become beneficial to yourself, to your family, to your loved ones, your kids, or anyone else in your life who has meaning to you. We sometimes forget that success and getting to it does not last forever. The reality is we're getting older every single day, and with getting older comes change. If you're a young person reading this book, just remember: the energy that you have today may not be there tomorrow. The drive that you have today may not be there tomorrow, so the wise thing to do is to make your money work for you. So when you're not able to get out here and hustle and make it happen, your money will make it happen for you. This thing called life can be really rewarding. This thing called life can be super challenging. This thing called life can be painful at times. This thing called life can be disappointing at times. But there's one thing that everyone can relate to: this thing called life is controlled and affected by day-to-day decision-making, and those decisions most of the time determine how your life will look down the road. Today is the start of a new day. No more turning back, it's time to move forward. It is time to flip these bricks! This time, as you flip bricks people's lives will change for the good. You will be providing a place for families to enjoy and live while making money. And one last thing: grab a cup of tea, sit back and relax, or find a quiet place and get ready for the art of flipping bricks.

– **Clarence KD McNair**

WHAT IS GENERATIONAL WEALTH?

Wealth in itself can mean many different things for people. Some think of wealth as a state of mind, material things, cash, or things acquired that can be liquidated. For me, generational wealth will start with me! The first mistake I made was underestimating the importance of education. My wife, Dr. Parson and I are building an empire. It has to start with educating yourself. Does that mean you have to go to college? No, not necessarily. I didn't go to college, but I am a proud father of a college graduate. My son just recently graduated with a degree in mechanical engineering. My youngest son is also in college. He's studying to be a sports broadcaster; so, the importance of college was instilled in them. These opportunities will give them a leg up in terms of building their financial independence. The path I chose was real estate. I've been in the business for over 20 years, and I am working on building an empire. Generational wealth for me will be teaching my sons to hustle for themselves; where they don't have to work and depend on anyone else. Generational wealth will also be me passing my company on to my sons, and one day them passing it on to their children. I would like for the cycle to then keep continuing. Then each generation will in turn continue the cycle of building wealth!

I grew up in Indianapolis Indiana, home of the KKK. I grew up in between poverty and middle class—I was somewhere in between the two. I was motivated to get into real estate for money after seeing the first realtor I met in Georgia (the person who sold me a house). She lived such a lavish lifestyle and she encouraged me to sign up for the real estate course. I also knew I needed to secure a legitimate profession to make a better life. I didn't want to go back to hustling.

The difference between me and other realtors is my drive, background, and hustle mentality. I've always had a hustle mindset, so for me selling houses comes naturally. I've been selling and flipping things since I was in the sixth grade. Most realtors would've given up in the beginning because the money doesn't just fall in your lap, it takes hard work and time. I was discouraged in the beginning, but my natural drive was to keep pushing. I also have a natural eye for finding housing for my clients. After initially speaking with them, I can usually find homes they end up falling in love with. I also stand out because I have over a decade of experience in valuing homes for all the major banks in the country.

I have made millions in real estate and sold multi-million-dollar homes for years. I sell homes to celebrities, thus earning the title "The Celebrity Realtor" #nosalarycap.

IMAGE AND PERCEPTION GOES A LONG WAY

Whether flipping houses or selling real estate, believe it or not, your image and the way people perceive you goes a hell of a long way.

I have known this since my early days as a hustler. When people used to see me in nice cars and clothes or dope jewelry, they would want to be a part of what I had going on! Now, in the day of social media, it's even more important. I can't tell you how many deals I have got just because people wanted to deal with me because I look successful, or they saw me driving a certain car or saw me with different designers on my back. It sounds crazy but it's true. Hence, sometimes if I'm buying a flip and an agent looks at the contract and sees my name, they choose my offers just because they want to work with me from my image that I have put out. From the beginning I always felt like if look like success it would come to me, so always look the part! It will take you a long way.

THE 10 FLIPPING BRICKS COMMANDMENTS

1. Cash is king when purchasing homes to flip.

2. Stay away from neighborhoods with tons of rental homes.

3. Always keep multiple hard money lenders, you may need more than one.

4. Always run comps on your potential flip.

5. Always keep the wholesaling option in mind if you find yourself in over your head, or you already have projects going on.

6. Always go into your deals with a clear understanding of your renovation cost.

7. Always take mold issues seriously.

8. Always check and see how long utilities have been off at an empty property. If you have electrical or gas repairs and it has been off, you could have major issues.

9. Learn how to do small jobs like install light fixtures and electrical wall plates, etc. It can save you a few dollars.

10. Find a great real estate closing attorney and stick with them. You will need one for any title issues you have, they can squeeze you in if you have last minute closings, and they can explain any legal issues.

FINDING GOOD CONTRACTORS IS ESSENTIAL WHEN FLIPPING BRICKS

I can't express how important it is to have good contractors when flipping houses. A bad contractor could kill all of your potential profits! One of the best ways to really find good contractors is by referral. A lot of times new investors will get family members and friends to help them with their projects after work and on the weekends. This typically ends up in disaster, because if you use family, you're usually paying them a low wage, and after they figure out it's real work, they will stiff you or drag your renovation out, which will cost you money. Friends on the other hand, if they have other jobs, will be tired when they get off work, and want to relax on the weekends, and you have also given them a minimum pay wage. So again, get real contractors. The most you want family and friends to help out with is hanging a ceiling fan or putting on some door knobs or something. Real talk.

Another thing: always get three estimates for repairs. Never go with the first estimate. It could be super high or so low that you know they can't do the work for that price. A good way to find good contractors is at Home Depot. They have a preferred contractor list; they are typically pretty good. Another nugget is, when you are riding around and you see contractors working on homes and they look like they are doing a good job, stop, let them know what you do and get a card from them. You can never have enough good contractors.

Never pay a contractor all their money before the job is complete: they will start focusing on their other projects and start working kind of slow on yours.

Always do a contract with your contractors. If you don't, you are sure to argue over money and repair disputes. With the contract there is no gray area.

One of my pet peeves is also contractors cleaning up after themselves at the end of a workday. I don't care if they do great work, I don't care if they are cheap, clean up after your damn self is what I preach! There is a fine in my contracts for leaving the projects dirty at the end of the day, and I also express to the contractors in the beginning that I am anal about it, so it won't be a surprise when I start ranting about it.

A great way to keep a good contractor close to you is to give him the price that he asks for if its fair and give him a tip if he does an excellent job.

While writing this book, one of my best contractors of 15 years passed away of Covid 19. RIP Mr. Errol. He saved me thousands of dollars over the years.

DESIGNING
YOUR FLIP

Outside of the price, what really sells a home is its design. The design of your home is essential when selling your flip. You want the design to grab people's attention while still being able to appeal to a broad range of people. Creating a great design includes selecting the right paint colors, flooring, finishes, hardware, etc. The cost allocated to the designs are directly related to the price point for resale and your budget. For instance, for a million-dollar home, a buyer may expect to see quartz countertops or Viking appliances. Spending a large amount for those things wouldn't make sense in a house that may sell for $200k.

Before you start, decide what design style you'd like to do for the house. Will it be modern, traditional, rustic, etc.? Then it's time to work on building your design palette for the house. I like to start with the flooring in the main area of the home, then decide on the kitchen cabinets, lighting, appliances, countertops, paint color, and the backsplash last. Sometimes I pick the fixtures based on a particular item

I want to use. I may have fallen in love with a particular vanity or mosaic tile, so I would find items with the budget that would complement it. There's not necessarily a right or wrong, but the most important thing is to make sure they all work together before moving forward. You may have fallen in love with a particular paint color you want to design a room after. Whatever your inspiration is, just make sure it all is aligned with the overall room/project.

Now that you're ready to start buying materials, let's not forget that nothing is purchased without having the budget in mind. Never compromise your budget due to a design choice. The budget is directly correlated to your profit, and you're doing this to make money, right? When selecting flooring, tiles, countertops, cabinets, etc., I recommend getting a few samples of each. Typically, you'll be selecting items from several different stores, so before you purchase all of the material needed, get a sample of each so that you can look at them all together. Sometimes, when you look at items individually, it can appear that things may match; however, that can change when they're presented together. It's a tip that can save you money in the long run or prevent unnecessary product returns.

Color Choices

Picking the right color can be all the change a room may need. The right color will enhance the feel of the room. The color can be as dramatic or as muted as you'd like. The great thing about color is that it's an easy change and fix if you're not happy. The first step would be identifying the color family you'd like to be in. If you have existing furniture, keep in mind how the color will complement the furniture. If you still need to pick out furniture, then consider how easy or difficult it could be to complement the color you chose. In either case, it's best to pick your favorite two or three colors, get a sample of each, and test it out on the wall. This may seem like an unnecessary step but in the end, it will save you a lot of time and reassure you that you've made the right choice.

Staging

Staging a home is the process of renting furniture to display in the home as if it was already occupied. Staging is a great tool to help sell the property. There are companies that will come look at the space and suggest and provide furnishings for an agreed upon amount of time for a cost. Although some people love the way you've designed the home, there are some who still won't have the vision to see the potential in the property. Staging aids with that. If there's room in the budget, staging can definitely enhance the sale of the property.

– Tiffany Veney, Madison Street Designs

PROS AND CONS OF INVESTING IN REAL ESTATE

Single family residences
- Pro: Smaller units for new flippers
- Con: less profit

Multi-unit properties
- Pro: More profit
- Con: More work and will entail much more expertise

Townhouses
- Pro: Smaller unit that's less area to fix up
- Con: May be less profit

HOA (Homeowners Associations)
- Con: May not allow renting, so check that first

Condominiums
- Pro: Smaller unit
- Con: May be less profit

It would be best for an investor to start off with residential. Most commercial spaces are much larger than residential, and you have to deal with zoning regulations depending on what type of establishment will be started there. The price point is way higher.

ARE YOU LOOKING TO RAISE YOUR SCORE TO PURCHASE A HOME?

Disclaimer: The information contained in this chapter is not a substitute for legal, financial, accounting or other advice. The general information provided is not a replacement or substitute for advice from a personal finance adviser. You should always seek the advice of professionals who are aware of and can advise you based on your personal financial situation and history. The information provided is general in nature and does not guarantee any specific results.

Here is a list of educational tips we provide to our clients. These tips have been very effective with increasing the credit score.

As I built up my reputation in the credit repair industry, I eventually began to learn different methods in increasing credit scores. I became great at leveraging the law to force credit bureaus to remove negative information they were unable to document from my report. Even with all this experience, though, I would from time to time still stumble upon single techniques so powerful, that it's hard to believe they exist. Rapid re-scoring, paying bills on time, paying down debt, keeping old accounts open are a few procedures, and if you've ever wondered how to raise your credit score, it could be something for you. Below is a list of methods to increase your score.

Rapid re-score with mortgage lenders

This method is used when you are trying to buy a home. With this strategy, the lender will review your credit report and tell you which item needs to be paid off or fixed. You will then pay off the negative items and get proof from the creditor. You then give the proof to the lender, who will give it to the third-party vendor, who passes the information to the credit bureau. The bureau will then update your credit report reflecting your new credit score. This strategy is used, primarily, when you are trying to get a home. This feature is offered by a third-party vendor, and the company is contracted by the credit bureau. The service is not offered to the public, only to mortgage brokers.

Pay your bills on time

Make a list of all your debts and their due dates. Then, type the due dates into your computer and cell phone calendars with active reminders. Use an Internet banking program and your online credit card site to send email reminders when your bills are due. In addition, you can set up your accounts to have money automatically taken out at the due date. When paying your bills, you can pay them as they come in using online banking or bill pay or through your financial institution website. Using the various methods mentioned above will help you pay your debts on time. Making each payment on time raises your credit score and keeps you in good standing with your creditors in case you request a credit increase.

Pay down your debt

Put your debts in order from the card with the highest balance to the lowest. Pay each account down to 7% to 10% and keep it there to increase your score. Finding money to help you pay down your debt may be difficult, but there are numerous ways to raise extra cash. You can have a garage sale, sell items on eBay, get an extra job, pull from your savings, borrow from friends, and cut your expenses. Any of these are an option.

Don't close old accounts

Closing tradelines won't help. In fact, it will hurt your score by reducing your total available credit and make your balances seem higher. It also makes your total credit look young, and the FICO model likes to see age on accounts because of payment history. Last, you want to keep the cards active by having a monthly bill debited from your card at the end of the month to prevent the creditor from closing your account due to lack of use. Most lenders will close inactive accounts after 18 months if the card is not being used.

Ask for a credit increase

Ask your creditor to raise your credit limit to reduce your balance. This will help raise your score slightly. Only do this if the balances of your other credit cards are low.

Apply for credit sparingly

Don't apply for many accounts in a short period of time because the credit bureaus will send a Trans Alert to the creditors informing them that you have applied for multiple accounts.

Re-aging

Ask your creditor to re-age your account to improve your credit score. This method is the process by which your creditor agrees to forgive your late payment history and reclassify your account as up to date. You must qualify for re-aging, according to the Federal Financial Institutions Examination Council (FFIEC) and establish and follow a policy that requires you to demonstrate a renewed willingness and ability to repay the debt. The account must be at least nine months old, and you must make three consecutive, monthly payments.

Your credit score

A credit score of 720 opens the doors to all credit, and a score of 500 closes the door to all credit. A 651 gets you qualified and a 700 opens the door to additional programs.

Have the credit bureaus add new accounts

Ask the credit bureau to add any account with a payment history that is not reflected on your credit report.

Don't pay off old debts to collectors

Paying off outdated, negative bills can actually hurt your score by renewing the date of the last activity of the debt and making it current. If the debt is close to falling off of your credit report, according to the Fair Credit Reporting Act Statute, then just let it come off on its own.

Your true credit card balance

If you know that your credit card balance is lower than what the credit bureau is showing, write the credit card company and have them update your credit card balance with the credit bureaus so that your score will increase.

How to Get Credit: Three Proven Ways to Build Credit Fast

Whether you are just starting out or simply trying to repair your record, you might be wondering how to get credit. Here are a few simple ways to get credit for the first time or during the rebuilding stage.

- **Get a Co-signer with Good Credit:** There's an old saying about the lottery: you can't win if you don't play. This is true in terms of credit, as well. You cannot get a loan if you never apply for a credit card or loan. If you currently have zero credit or it is bad, you may need a co-signer with a good record to apply with you. This co-signer adds their name to your card or loan, meaning if you fail to pay your bills, they are as responsible as you are.

- **Apply for a Secured Credit Card:** If a co-signer is not available to help you get a loan, you may be required to put down a security deposit before you are given a card. Usually, this amount will be the same as the credit you are requesting. If you fail to make your payments, the credit card company will take what is owed out of your deposit and report it negatively to the reporting agencies.

- **Start Good Financial Habits:** The better financial habits you keep now, the more likely you are to be offered and approved to get a loan later. This means paying all your bills on time, paying off as much of your debts each month as possible, and not reaching your maximums by routinely utilizing less than 6% of your limit.

Now that you are empowered with additional information, go out there and take action to start building your financial life.

The information that is provided was taught by my mentor. I'm thankful for having him as a credit business mentor.

On behalf of Platinum Superior Solutions LLC, we are proud to provide you with educational resources and services that can help you reach your goals. If you need help with your credit, our website is www.superiorsolutionsusa.com, and our contact number is 404-383-1082. We will be happy to assist you with your financial goals. Mention this book and get a list of our credit builders for free!

Let's get you into a home!

WHAT ARE HARD MONEY LOANS?

Hard money loans, or what I refer to as private money loans, are an integral part of the real estate investment industry. While traditional banking institutions are known to serve developers, builders and investors on a large scale, private money fills the huge gap filled by smaller investors, as well as providing incremental funding for large, seasoned real estate companies.

Private money loans are typically asset-based loans, meaning the real estate securing the loan is the key component to the transaction and funding. Lenders first and foremost want to know that the value of the collateral is adequate to support the risk the lender is taking. That is not to say we don't look at the principals or borrowers, because their experience and investment in the transaction is also critical – especially when we are looking to build a long-term relationship.

Loans from private lenders are easier to obtain than traditional bank loans, and can close much quicker, making them advantageous to wholesalers, property flippers and investors. A quick close can be a factor in winning a bidding war and in getting more favorable purchase terms, as the shorter close time gives sellers more comfort. The cost of a private loan is more expensive than other sources, but the benefits of a local, accessible lender who can close quickly frequently outweighs the additional expense.

Raise Your Credit Score Fast Track

Pay Your Bills On Time
- Never be late
- Use payment reminders
- Bring accounts current

Pay Down Your Balances
- Pay balances down to 7%
- Pay high interest credit cards fast
- Get a second job or sell items on ebay

Length of Credit
- Never close old account
- Ask creditors to re-open old account
- Keep old account active

Mix of Credit
- Keep a mixture of tradelines
- 5 different trade lines at one time
- Credit card, loan, retail card

New Credit
- Apply for new credit card once every 6 months
- More than 2 inquires in 6 months can hurt your score
- Inquiries only affect your score for 12 months

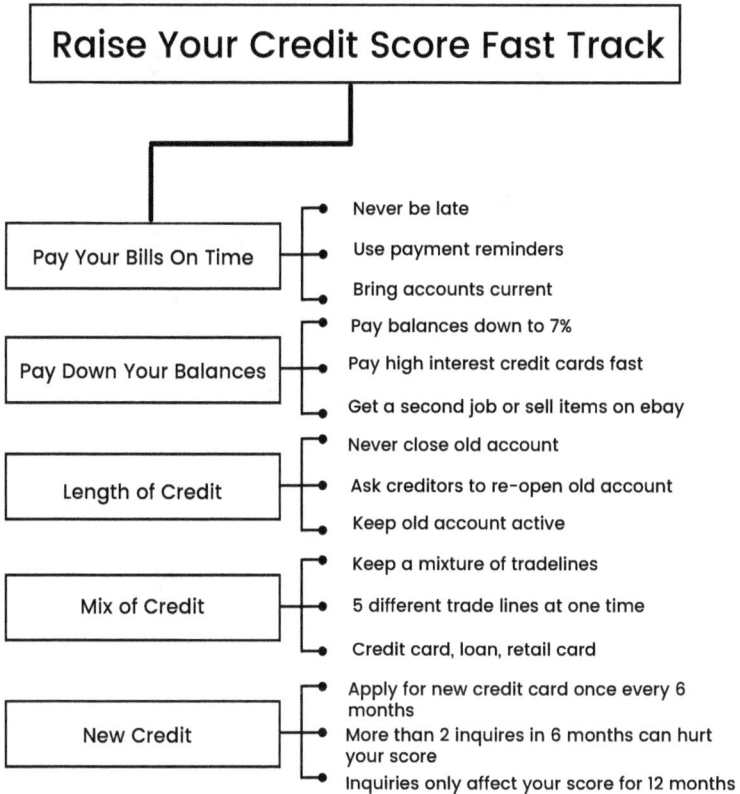

-Tiana Williams, Credit Specialist

ADVICE FOR
FLIPPING HOUSES...

1. If you want to flip houses, it's a good idea to get your real estate license, because you can make commissions off of homes you purchase. You can save money when you sell, because you can be the listing agent.

2. If you are going to flip houses, you need mentorship.

3. If you are going to get your real estate license, do not quit your day job when you first start (success will not happen overnight).

4. Good credit is key when flipping houses. Example: restoration of the homes can be made with Home Depot or Lowes cards.

5. Unless you are paying cash, you will typically need a hard money lender. Consult with a few to see who has the best rates for borrowing money.

6. Find two or three handymen that are local to utilize for flip repairs to save money from using a traditional contractor.

7. Find a seasoned agent to locate undervalued properties.

8. Learn how to navigate Craigslist, Amazon, and eBay for discounted renovation materials.

9. Always try to buy homes that you are flipping in areas with good schools.

10. When selling your flip, one thing to know is that unless your buyer has cash or is getting a conventional loan, you will have to hold the property for at least 90 days for FHA loans.

11. When flipping, if you are a cash buyer, you can save a ton of money going to your local county foreclosure sales.

12. Never cut costs on landscaping when flipping. That's one of the first things a potential buyer will see.

13. When flipping, search for houses seven days a week, because there's a lot of people out there doing the same thing.

14. When flipping, always know what similar homes have sold for in the last three to nine months in the immediate area (pull your comparable).

15. Find one thing that you can do on your own to cut costs: trash out, landscaping, etc.

16. Find a good closing attorney to avoid title and lean issues.

17. Having your own pickup truck will save you money and time.

18. Always get homeowners insurance on your flip. Do not try and save money: it can be disastrous.

19. In regard to securing your materials, always be aware of the areas you are flipping in. Not so good area, don't leave materials out.

20. When flipping, try to find homes that are near where you live. This will save travel time daily.

21. When buying flips, pay attention to master bedroom sizes and bathrooms count.

22. A simple business card will go a long way when flipping. It helps to let people know what you do.

23. Ride around different neighborhoods and look for distressed looking properties. Get the address, pull tax records, and send a letter to see if they would like to sell.

24. Always overestimate for repairs on your flip. It will save you money in the end.

25. Never do your deals verbally or with a handshake. Get everything in writing!

THINGS NOT TO DO
BEFORE A DEAL

1. Do not buy another house while you're under contract. If you are buying cash, this will be okay. If not, your purchase will affect your debt ratio and credit score.

2. Do not apply for any new credit cards. This will affect your credit score, and this could cause your score to go below the lender requirements.

3. Do not cosign for any loans. This will affect your credit, and if the signer is late making a payment, this will affect your credit as well.

4. Do not apply for an auto loan. Applying for an auto loan will cause your credit score to go down, and if it's a soft pull, this could affect your ability to make the home purchase.

5. Do not do any repairs to the property you are buying until you close on the property. You will not want to do this, because if you do not close on the property for some reason, you will not be reimbursed for any money spent.

6. Do not pass on your opportunity to do a property inspection. Property inspections are important, because although it may seem to be perfect there are a plethora of potential hidden issues you can't see with the bare eye. These things could be extremely costly.

7. Do not deplete your bank account prior to closing. This is a serious matter! You will need to have veri-fiable funds to close your deal. If you don't and you pull the money from other places, that will cause a lot of red tape explanations. If you deplete your account prior to closing, you will not have seasoned money in your account. These are funds that have been in your account for a period of time.

8. Do not max any credit cards out. This will affect your score and debt to income ratio.

9. When renovating homes, don't underestimate your potential repairs. Always overestimate and have extra revenue set aside, because when you underestimate

and the repairs are more, you may have to cut corners.

10. Don't overestimate your personal skills to complete repairs in the property. For example, just because you can change a light bulb, this doesn't mean you can install the actual light. In this case it could cause death.

11. Do not go into the flip without a cost budget. You want a cost budget, because you want to know every single estimated cost for the repairs. If you don't, you could end up with a lot of incomplete repairs. This could affect the sale of your flip.

12. Do not forget to calculate your carrying cost. These are monthly bills for the flip. Include mortgage, utilities, etc. This is separate from your repair budget costs.

13. Do not overpay for a flip. If you overpay for a flip, you could end up putting a lot of time and effort into a project that will not give you a return in the end. Meaning, you will only break even, and not make a profit.

14. Do not miss the chance to get multiple estimates for repairs. You need multiple estimates for your flips, because two good contractors could have totally different estimates. Of course, if they produce the same level of work, you want to go with the cheapest.

15. Do not move any of your repair materials into a property before you close. You don't know who has access to the property, and you could have your materials stolen.

16. Never buy a flip without doing a final walk through before closing. Sometimes when dealing with flips, especially in urban areas, there are break-ins. Security is sometimes an issue, and you don't want to buy and go back to a vandalized property. Examples: missing fixtures (lights, fans, etc.)

17. Don't forget to check crime in the immediate area. Knowing the level of security needed is important. Example, do you need security doors or an alarm?

18. Do not forget to estimate for landscaping. One of the first things you see when pulling up to a property is the exterior and landscaping. If the landscaping doesn't look good, the potential buyers could decide to move on. First impressions are important!

19. Do not take advice from a non-flipper about your flip. You want advice from someone with expertise, and not someone who doesn't have the experience to adequately advise you.

20. Do not underestimate the crime in the area, it could be costly. If you are in a high crime area, always consider alarm systems and security doors.

21. Do not tell other flippers about yours until you are under contract or closed. You don't want to tell other flippers about your potential projects. They could go behind your back with cash and purchase the property.

22. Do not use comps that are over a year old to decide on value. Comps are other properties that are similar to your potential buy. You don't want to use old comps, because the market value typically changes every two to three months.

23. Do not ever plan to do electrical work on your flip, it could cost you your life. Once again, if you do not have the experience and / or certification to do this, it could be deadly. Hire an experienced electrician.

24. Never tell a potential buyer your exact sale price prior to completing all work. You may end up spending more than expected on your project, and there will be an issue with the potential buyer if you change the price.

25. Never opt out of an Appraisal opportunity. You will always want to know the current value of a home, and this is so you do not overpay for a property.

THINGS THAT COULD GO WRONG THE WEEK BEFORE YOUR CLOSING DAY

1. You could lose your job.

2. An old tax lien can pop up on your credit.

3. A buyer or seller can get cold feet and not want to buy or sell the property they're under contract on.

4. Title issues may occur.

5. The house could catch fire or be vandalized.

6. You could get a low-ball appraisal and have major issues.

7. Your cash to close could go up for whatever reason and you don't have reserves for the increase, etc.

THE CLOSING PROCESS

So, you've found your dream home and put it under contract. Congratulations! The real estate contract will tell all parties how long the buyer has to turn in their money to the escrow holder in the transaction, which in Georgia is most likely the closing attorney. The closing attorney's role in a real estate transaction is to pull the title to the property, examine and clear it, and issue a title insurance policy. In addition to this, the closing attorney is most likely the escrow agent, and they collect and disburse funds as they relate to a particular transaction.

Once a contract is submitted to the closing attorney's office, it is thoroughly reviewed, and important deadlines are identified. After the earnest money deposit is received in by the closing attorney or holder, there is a legally enforceable contract between the parties, and the attorney will then order the title. Once a title search is performed, the attorney is able to see the condition of the title: Who the current owner is, and any encumbrances or defects in the title. Once identified, the attorney then works to clear the title, before issuing a title insurance policy. This title insurance policy is for the benefit of the buyer and protects the buyer from any flaw or misstep in the title work performed by the attorney.

Title insurance is really important, and, just like car insurance and health insurance, you don't need it until you need it. For example, if there was an encumbrance missed on the title search and report, and there ended up being a person with a greater right to title than you, this person would be able to take your home, or an interest in the land that your home sits on. If you'd purchased a title insurance policy in this instance, then you would be able to use your policy to be made whole. Without the title insurance policy, the other party, assuming they were in title, could be entitled to your home, or to interest in the land your home sits on. So yes, it's better to be safe than sorry! It is absolutely prudent to purchase title insurance. It is worth every penny, every single time.

The attorney's office will be in contact with both the buyer and seller during the closing process. It is very important to return all information sheets to the closing attorney as soon as possible. The information collected is used to verify information and it assists the attorney in particularizing each client's file in the operating system. The attorney will reach out to both parties of the transaction as much as needed to get required information to process the transaction.

The closing attorney works with the lender and on behalf of the lender (if the transaction involves a loan) to process the file through the closing process. Payoffs are ordered, homeowner association letters are ordered, and tax and utility bills are collected for, if necessary. The lender and the closing attorney collaborate until both of their figures balance with each other. Once this happens, the lender and the closing attorney can both produce the final documents that will be signed at the closing table.

Once the title has been cleared, and the loan has been cleared to close by the lender, the closing attorney will reach out to both parties to schedule a time for closing. If there are any funds to be collected from you by the closing attorney, it is prudent to send those funds to the closing attorney using a wire transfer from your bank the day before. This makes closing day easier, and it ensures that there will be no delays in the funding of the loan caused by you. Once arriving at the closing attorney's office, the attorney, or their staff, will get a copy of both parties' IDs, and then the signing will begin. Once all documents have been properly signed, and the lender has given funding authorization, the closing attorney disburses the transaction and makes sure all instruments are properly recorded (security deed, warranty deed, POA, etc.). The buyer gets keys to their home, and the seller gets proceeds. A true win–win situation!

The closing process can be a daunting one if you don't have the help of a real estate professional. At my closing firm SRS Title, LLC located in Dunwoody, GA, my staff and I pride ourselves on providing top tier settlement service to all of our clients. We will hold your hand all the way to the closing table, because sometimes, that's what it takes to get a transaction closed. Happy house hunting and happy closing!

– Kendra Robinson, Esq., Kendra Robinson and Associates, LLC

SURVIVING A FLIP FOR RESIDENTIAL RENOVATION

Understanding Your Goals

So, you think you're ready to do a rehab? Well, get ready, because it's a hell of a ride. Real Estate can have wonderful benefits, but like any industry, not every opportunity is a win. To be successful in real estate you must do your due diligence. Not every deal is a good one. The famous saying is totally correct: real estate revolves a lot around "location, location, location." There are several factors to consider before purchasing a house to flip. Some are obvious, like the condition or the price, but others are not, like what the renovation costs, holding costs, or changes in the market or resale value are. In this guide, we'll walk through the process of flipping a house and point out some things to look out for.

The first thing to consider when thinking about flipping a house is understanding your goal. Are you trying to do a quick flip? What kind of upgrades will be needed for the area the house is in? What happens if it doesn't sell? How much should you budget for the renovations? These are just a few questions we will tackle in this guide. Although there's no sure way to prevent a loss, there's a lot you can do to improve the odds of you scoring big or, worst case, breaking even.

This renovation will be your new baby, and just like with a new baby it comes with a rollercoaster of emotions. You'll be happy, sad, angry, anxious, excited, motivated, doubtful, discouraged—shit, you might even cry once or twice. I want you to understand that nearly every obstacle has a solution, so the plan is to focus on how to get to the finish line.

Deciding Where to Invest

Whether you're buying a home to reside in or an investment, location will always be on the top of the list when deciding where to purchase. You can start the home search process by identifying the upcoming transitional areas where you live. Your local city/county will typically list that information on their respective websites along with developmental plans. You typically want to be in an emerging area or sometimes you'll luck up on a property that's already located in an established neighborhood.

Once you find the area you want to invest in, it's time to look for the property that works for you. When you find that property, you'll need to research the following things:

- What similar properties in that area are selling for now
- The margin of profit for the property, by looking at the average sale price for the fully rehabbed property minus the asking price of the property you're interested in
- Look at what the homes sold for that are in the current condition of the house you'd like to purchase to make sure you're not overpaying
- Estimate the cost of repairs. Later we can discuss if you want to make the basic repairs based on those comps or if you'll spend more on the repairs in order to get a higher asking price
- How long are properties staying on the market when listed?

Deciding on Financing Options

How you plan on paying for the property and renovations also plays a role in the project. Are you using cash, financing along with cash, renovation loan, or a private hard money loan?

Cash

- Buying with cash gives you bargaining power

- Sellers are more attracted with cash offers because it usually guarantees a quicker closing, and they don't have to worry about any delays from the bank

- Sellers will often take a lower asking price when offered a cash deal

- Sellers will require POF (Proof of Funds) to make sure you're able to close the deal prior to accepting the offer so make sure your documents are ready

Financing and with Cash

- The first step will be getting approved by a lender. That amount will determine how much buying power you have

- With this option, the loan will cover the purchase of the home, but you will need to use your personal finances to pay for the renovations

- Before proceeding with this option, you MUST consult with at least two contractors to get a good idea of the renovation costs. If the quotes aren't close to each other, get a third opinion, and go with the average of all three to get a good idea of the renovation costs, and add another 15%-20% to allow room for unexpected costs

Renovation (203k) Loan

- A renovation loan is where a bank loans you money for the purchase of the home and money for the renovation. There are different types of renovation loans

- The bank requires a bid on the work from a licensed contractor of your choice. That bid will need to fit within the amount the bank is willing to allocate for the renovation. For instance, if the bank will give you $100,000 for renovation, they will not accept a bid over that amount

- The bank also won't allow you to pay for repairs outside of the loan or allow you to build in sweat equity

- Each lender may have different guidelines, so it's best to review them prior to closing. You want to make sure the renovation plans you have for the flip won't be constricted by those guidelines

- The bank requires that the repairs are done on a draw schedule and that a third-party draw inspection before payment can be made at each stage

Private Hard Money Loan

- A hard money loan is when a private person or lender agrees to lend you money to buy the property and the funds to complete the renovations

- Hard money loans usually have a high interest rate

- Like a renovation loan that will disperse money based on a draw schedule (see attached example)

- The hard money lender may do the draw inspections themselves or require that a third-party is paid to make sure the work was completed before the funds are dispersed

- You'll likely be required to front some of the renovation costs and/or pay a fee to initiate the loan and pay a fixed monthly amount during the renovation

Analyzing the Value of the Property

The value of the property, simply put, is what it's worth. To determine the value of the property you need to look at the comparables within the last three to six months. That means looking at properties that sold with the same or similar characteristics, like number of bedrooms, square footage, condition, number of bathrooms, and proximity to the subject property. You want to determine the current price people are willing to pay for the property once it's been updated. You should also research the average price the homes have sold for based on the current condition of the property. The difference between the two prices gives you the range to use to determine your profit margin, so the more you spend to fix up the home, the less that number is.

Developing a Budget

Budgets can make and break any deal. There should be at least a 15%–20% contingency built into your budget. There's ALWAYS the possibility of an unexpected expense when doing a rehab. You also need to factor in your carrying costs that will occur if you don't finish the repairs on time, delays with permits, if the property doesn't sell as quickly as expected. You should get two to three bids from contractors for your project. Make sure it's itemized, that way you can try to compare by trades. For instance, one plumbing total could be $9000 and another one could be $7000. It can help you negotiate the prices and/or help you determine how to cut or increase line items. You can also give the contractors your budget and see if they can do the work within those numbers. I would highly recommend knowing what your renovation costs are before purchasing the property. Ignoring this step can kill your profits and even cost you money. Take time to really look at how much you spend on fixtures, flooring, appliances, etc. It's easy to get caught up in "what looks nice." The finished product definitely sells the home, but you don't want to over-improve. Make sure that you're making your decisions within the budget you created. Use the example budget below to help you develop the budget for your project.

Total Project Budget: 14 Week Timeline	$ 200,000.00
Week 1	**$ 20,000.00**
Engineering Fees	$ 1,261.87
Electric permit	$ 300.00
Lumber Charges	$ 1,261.87
Waste Management Dumpster (delivered 13th)	$ 655.00
Clear debris from parking lot including trees	
Building Permit Fee	

Repair/Replace subfloor
Frame all rooms and bathrooms including
kitchen
Replace LVLs
Repair Roof
Frame windows

Week 2   **$ 15,000.00**
HVAC Rough-in
Install Windows

Inspections for 2nd Disbursement from Lender
Week 3   **$ 10,000.00**
Plumbing Rough-in

Week 4   **$ 10,000.00**
Electric Rough-in

Week 5   **$ 10,000.00**
Framing, Electrical, Plumbing, and HVAC
City inspections
Insulation

Inspections for 3rd Disbursement from Lender
Week 6   **$ 20,000.00**
**(Sprinkler installation will take place
this week)**

Week 7	**$ 10,000.00**
Fire System	
Flooring installed	$ 12,000.00
Window siding	$ 2,000.00
Front Extension demo	$ 1,000.00
Front Framing and enclosure	$ 9,000.00
Condensing Unit	$ 15,000.00
	$ 134,000.00

Inspections for 4th Disbursement from Lender

Week 8	**$ 15,000.00**
Drywall	

Week 9	**$ 10,000.00**
Drywall	

Week 11	**$ 8,000.00**
Interior/Exterior Doors	
Molding	
Interior paint	

Inspections for 5th Disbursement from Lender

Week 12	**$ 10,000.00**
Hot water tank	
Install Lighting	
	$ 5,000.00
Install Fixtures	

Inspections for 6th Disbursement from Lender

Week 14   **$ 6,000.00**

Occupancy Inspections

**Inspection days are not included in the work schedule. For example, if the plumbing inspection takes a week, that does not affect the contractor projected time by a week.

***This schedule is a living document that is subject to change at any time.

***Any delays by the contractor after 14 weeks will be at the expense of the contractor.

***Provided that all schedule deadlines are met, draw checks will be released on a weekly basis every Friday. If schedule deadlines are not met, then draw checks will be released once deadline has been met.

***Any materials purchased by the owner outside of the kitchen equipment will be reduced by the contractor draw amount.

OWNER SIGNATURE: _____

CONTRACTOR SIGNATURE: _____

This budget spreadsheet can be used to develop a timeline, outline the budget for each step, and determine when an inspection is needed by the lender and/or local governing agency. Some of the line items on the spreadsheet may only be pertinent to commercial properties or a large residential one.

Hiring a Contractor

Hiring a contractor is vital to the success of your project. Not only do you want someone with the appropriate skillset, you want them to be professional, reliable, accountable and aware of their spending. Unfortunately, contractors do have a bad reputation of exceeding the budget or leaving a project before its completion. When selecting a contractor, try to get a referral from someone you trust, if possible. Before you make a final decision, I would speak to at least two to three contractors, review the scope of work, request a bid, vet the provided referrals, and go look at some of their projects in person if possible.

You should also take into consideration how you engaged with the contractor. You'll be working closely with this person and their team, so you want to make sure it's a person you think you will mesh well with. Set the tone for your project in the beginning to make sure that your objectives are aligned with the contractor that you choose.

Here are a few questions you can ask the contractor during the interview:

1. How many projects are you managing right now?

2. Are you licensed and insured?

3. How many people are on your team?

4. Can you dedicate 5–6 days to my project a week? If not, how many days a week would be allocated to my project?

5. Are you able to pull all the permits needed for the project?

6. Do you foresee any obstacles that could lead to a delay in the project?

7. Do you think you're usually under or over budget with your projects? Explain.

8. How would you communicate with me to make sure I'm consistently up to date with the progress of the project?

9. How would you handle an unexpected repair or a change that needed to be made?

10. Do you have any current or recent projects that I can visit to see your work?

11. What amount do you require for a deposit? How do you prefer to be paid?

Make sure you and your contractor sign a contract that identifies in detail the scope of the project, the budget, and the timeline. I recommend adding a clause that states stipulations if the timeline is missed.

Preparing for the Renovation

Before you start construction, there are a few things you can start preparing for. Since you're the new owner of the property, you will need to transfer the gas and electric service to you or your business name. If the property was vacant or a complete gut, then you'll actually need to apply for a new account. This process is very extensive and could take months! You'll also need to check to see if you need a water and/or sewer account and apply for it if so. Permits can also take a few weeks to be issued. You should have the demolition permit before starting any work. It would make sense to try to have the building permit as well, as that's the next work that will be performed after the demolition. If you're changing the structural make up to the house (i.e. an addition, reframing a window or exterior door, replacing several joists, rafters, etc.), then you'll be required to provide additional information when submitting your building permit application. Review the requirements with your local governing agencies to determine if you'll need architectural drawings, a structural engineer, or any other documentation.

Permits

There are several permits that are generally needed during a renovation. Each municipality differs in determining what permit is needed dependent on the level of work being performed. For instance, you'll need a permit to replace an electrical panel, but you may not need one to replace a few outlets. Permits ensure that the work is being done based on the standards set by the local governing agency. It's important to know that permits have an expiration date, so make sure all inspections are passed under that permit prior to the expiration, or an extension is applied for if needed prior to the expiration. If not, you will be required to apply for a new permit, incurring additional fees and possible delays.

- Demolition: this covers the demolition work performed during the project. It covers the removal of drywall, flooring, joists, appliances, fixtures, etc. There are different types of demolition permits based on what or how much is being removed, i.e. if any structural components are being changed

- Building Permit: covers the structural integrity of the framing work, the subfloor, windows, doors, insulation

- Plumbing: covers all your plumbing related work. Adding/repairing plumbing lines, water heaters, water lines to all the fixtures, line to the septic system, etc.

- Electrical: covers the electrical work performed in the renovation. It covers running electrical wires throughout the project, electrical panel work, electrical outlets, low/high voltage wires, light fixtures, fans, stove, etc.

- HVAC: covers the work performed on the heating and cooling system. This includes the duct work, the furnace, AC unit, baseboard heaters, etc.

- Structural: usually requires an architect. This covers work that alters the structural integrity of the home.

This is related to the number of joists replaced, any new door openings or window openings, and/or any changes to the roof

- Use & Occupancy: deems that the house is suitable to live in based on the codes established by the local ordinances. This may entail two different inspections, one from the fire department and one from the building inspection. If the house was classified as vacant prior to the remodel, then they would need to come certify that its now habitable. Therefore, it would change the home from vacant to a single family, detached, row home, etc.

Almost all permits require an inspection to confirm that the work was performed to code. For example, if you pulled a plumbing permit for a full renovation job, then the first inspection needed would be for a "rough-in." Rough-in means the initial running of the pipes, wires, etc. are performed. So, for plumbing it would be running the lines to the septic system, to the water heater, the lines for the tubs, toilets, showers, sinks, etc. This has to be inspected while the walls are still open to make sure it's done to code before the walls can be closed and fixtures are actually attached to the lines.

Establishing a Timeline

In a perfect world everyone's project could be completed asap. While you can certainly have an expected timeframe to complete the project, it's imperative to make sure that timeline is obtainable with the contractor. There should also be time incorporated within the timeline to allow for unexpected delays. Two things that aren't under your control that directly affect your timeline would be material availability or inspections. Due to shifts in material availability since the COVID pandemic started, I recommend buying as many materials ahead of your project start date as possible. It's impossible to determine which material will fall short next, so it'll be much easier to find a small percentage of what you need as opposed to the entire consignment. Although the code for a trade can be "clear," every inspection really depends on the inspector doing the inspection. If the inspector requires a change, big or small, it could cause several delays with completing the request and rescheduling the inspection. In some cases, it may not be a complete stop on the project. For example, if you failed the electrical rough-in inspection while you're making the corrections, you could still be working on the plumbing rough-in.

Design That Shit

Let design be the fun part of the project! The flipping process can be stressful enough, so this should be the part that's stress-free. For the main flooring area, I would suggest going with a nice clean neutral choice. Gray is very popular and depending on the location is usually a great choice. If the homes in the area are more traditional, a light tan wood color flooring would work. Keep in mind that you're designing for the masses. Try to make sure each room has some type of focal point, even if its subtle. It could be the tile or the vanity if it's a bathroom, for the kitchen maybe it's the countertops, the living room could be the fireplace, etc.

Consider molding designs in your project. They're very diverse and can be used for a wall or ceiling design. There's a ton of online resources you can use to help you narrow down a design. Don't reinvent the wheel if you don't have to. What if you hate the design process or just feel stuck? Consider hiring a professional. Designers are creatives, so that means they generally consider their designs art. If you hire a designer, don't forget that you hired them because you liked their previous designs. Because of that, make sure to give the designer room to design. The designer is there to make your life easier, so let them.

Preparing to List the Property

During the process, it's important to check the comps every few weeks to make sure there hasn't been a drastic or even a consistent shift in the market. The goal is to sell the property fast and for the most amount of money possible. You want the house to have some "wow" factors that will draw the potential buyer in. You must get people interested in seeing the property, and that's done by taking great pictures of some of the main parts of the house. You want to take enough pictures to pique the buyer's interest and make them want to come out. The pictures are vital, but the price is equally vital. If the property is priced too much over the market value, then it could deter people from coming. In a sellers' market, where there's low inventory and the seller has an upper hand, you are likely to be able to list over market price and still maintain the traffic. In a buyer's market, the inventory is high, so the buyer has the upper hand, so you want to make sure the property is priced at or slightly below market rate to funnel traffic to the house. Listing the house under market value is usually done to increase traffic and create a situation with multiple offers, which will drive the price over market value. There's a risk with doing that, however, so you should make sure you evaluate the market properly prior to deciding what to list the price for. Whatever price you choose, you will have to keep in mind the cost of the renovation and the fees that will need to come out of that price, as well to determine your profit margin. In almost all cases, the seller will pay the commission for their agent and the buyer's agent. Be sure to review what those numbers are with the agent prior to listing the house. These figures could be negotiated; however, if the commission is too low, it could deter agents from wanting to show the property to their clients. Pricing the property is also a risk, because it can cause the property to sit longer without any offers.

Going into the project, you should've already had a listing price in mind. You should also be following the market while the rehab is taking place. By the end of the project, when it's time to list the property, your listing price should still be in the original range you had in mind. Your agent will likely have a marketing strategy in mind to attract potential buyers as well. There are a lot of ways to attract buyers, like open houses, online ads, staging, etc. Make sure you know your agents plan and that it's something you're comfortable with. Keep in mind that some options incur additional costs so that will be an additional expense to you in most cases.

What Happens When Shit Hits the Fan

What could go wrong? ANYTHING!!! The number one thing to know and understand before you even buy a property is that anything can go wrong. You can't have the mindset that everything will go as planned or that you won't run into any unexpected costs. On Day 1 of demo, you can open up the wall and find joists that are deteriorating. Your budget may have called just to replace one or two for $1,000, but now you have a $6,000 issue. If something like this happens, you should have money in your contingency to cover it, but you should still think of ways to get that money back if possible. For instance, maybe you were going to get a fancy hand railing inside for $5,000. Well, now you may have to settle for a more standard one that may cost $1,500. In order to be successful and last in real estate investing, you must be resilient, flexible, and able to problem solve.

What if I have an issue with my contractor? Ask yourself if the issue can be managed without severing the relationship. Changing the contractor should be your last resort, but it can be done. There may be financial losses, work delays, permit delays, etc. because of this decision. This is business, but we're still all humans. So, knowing how to talk to people in order to get what you need done is key. In the worst-case scenario, if the contractor hasn't done the work they were paid to do, or if it wasn't up to code, you could file a claim against them. You can contact the board they're licensed with and or start a claim with your local small claims court. These are not immediate fixes, so you need to make sure whatever decision you make will have the least negative effect on your overall project.

RENOVATION COMPLETION CHECKLIST

Permits		Drywall	
Building		Hanging Sheetrock	
Architectural Plans		Mudding and Taping	
Electrical			
Plumbing		**Paint**	
Mechanical		Interior Walls	
Demolition		Doors	
Use & Occupancy		Exterior Surfaces	
Septic Tank Inspection			
Water Well Inspection		**Fixtures**	
		Bathroom Lights	
		Exhaust Fans	
Administrative		Tub/Shower Fixtures	
Apply for Gas/Electric		Vanities	
Apply for Water/Sewage		Toilets	
Order Dumpster		Appliances	
Order Porta Potty		Doors	

Land Survey		Kitchen Cabinets	
Zoning (If changing property USE)		Towel Bars	
		Toilet Paper Holder	
Framing			
2x4s			
LVL		**Flooring**	
Subfloor		Subfloor	
Windows		Tile	
Exterior Doors		Vinyl Planks	
Closets		Epoxy	
Plumbing Rough-In		**Finishings**	
Line to Septic Tank		Baseboard Molding	
Flange for Toilets		Door Stops	
Water Line for Toilet		HVAC returns/vents	
Shower/Tub Drain		Door Hardware	
Lines for Shower/Tub Fixtures		Cabinet Hardware	
Line for Dishwasher		Kitchen Backsplash	
Line for Garbage Disposal		Light Face Plates	
Line for Kitchen Sink		Outlet Covers	
		Exterior	
Mechanical		Gutters	

Duct Work		Downspouts	
Furnace		Roof	
Condensation Line		Landscaping	
		Driveway	
		Lighting	
Electrical Rough-In			
Panel Box			
Lines for Standard/GFCI Outlets			
Lines to Light Switches			
Lines for Ceiling Lights/Fans			
Outlet for Stove			
Outlet for Fridge			
Outlet for Dishwasher			
Outlet for Garbage Disposal			
Outlet/Line for Hood			
Outlet for Microwave			
Outlet for W/D			
Outlet for Furnace			
Outlet for AC Unit			
Outlet for Water Heater			
Lines for Exterior Outlets			
Lines for Exterior Lights			

– Madison

GET A PROPERTY MANAGER

When an investor purchases a property, they don't think as far as who will manage such a huge investment. The excitement of the bottom line—or better yet, the net operating income—is what matters with such a great investment to generate wealth. The most important part of this is always left out. Once a property closes, the next step needs to be addressed. PROPERTY MANAGEMENT, with managing an investment. You need to look at all angles and drill down into the expenditure for the investment. You must have a strong team to ensure that the property is not neglected in the long haul. Daily operations need to be handled accordingly. The team would consist of a property manager, leasing and maintenance to keep things afloat for the investment daily. You will have resident complaints, rent collections, annual inspections, capital expenses, repairs and maintenance, marketing, and administrative expenses to keep the property going. These key items are important for the day-to-day to get to that bottom line, the net operating income. Budgets are set, and any investor wants to keep the expenses down and stay within budget. This is where the property manager oversees the day-to-day operations to control the expenses. Any emergency can arise, and this is where Capital Expense comes into play. This is the reserve that is set for capital items that may exceed what is in a normal budget, such as roof replacements, painting, restriping and paving, exterior light, etc.

Capital items are big ticketed items that must be set because you will never know when these items will need to be replaced. Having a property management company to oversee your property is critical. The manager needs to understand how to plan efficiently and manage the time of the operations. It's definitely not a one man show. A team must be on the same page to ensure items are in stock for maintenance to make repairs in a unit. Maintenance must be efficient and manage their time accordingly, because emergencies do happen, and it can be at any given time. Inventory of supplies must be checked daily and ordered accordingly in a timely manner. A maintenance supervisor is normally the person that is responsible for tracking equipment, ordering of the supplies and making sure that the work orders are completed, and notes are documented so that the office staff can document these work orders into the software. If you ever need to revisit an issue, we have full documentation of what repairs were completed for any unit. In addition, statistics show that having a property management company to oversee your assets is valuable. The property manager understands the ins and out of the day-to-day operations. With dealing with residential communities, there are more details, their annual fire inspections, and license renewals, and you also must ensure that everything is up to code, which means you may have to pull permits for repairs. In the industry of property management, you have to know how to use your time wisely, because you will drown slowly. You have to be a strong manager to lead your team in the right direction. If the manager doesn't have it together and is not a strong leader, the team will not know what direction to go in.

Your leasing staff is also an important piece to the puzzle of owning a property. They are the ones that will deal in customer service, making sure the work orders are entered, putting together the renewals for leases that will expire, and in most states, a 60-day notice required to vacate, without being charged for insufficient notice to vacate. They are also the ones that will collect rent for the residents and make sure the delinquency is as low as possible. Leasing agents are the ones that will put the files together for new move in, renewals, eviction, and send files to collections for residents that have unpaid balances. Leasing agents also help with making sure the units are made ready for prospects that plan to move in. They must do inspections of the unit once maintenance has turned in the keys for them to review the unit before the renter moves in. Once they have inspected and the unit is in perfect condition, they can now get the lease prepared for the applicant, and make sure they have the keys ready for the move in. Leasing agents also assist the property manager of the daily operations, handle the complaints of the resident and make sure all work orders are handled in a timely manner. If work orders are not handled accordingly, it may cause more damage to a unit and even affect other units. So, all work orders need to be placed in the system, because we are all human and may forget to handle the situation for the resident. This can cause turnover of losing a resident if we do not take care of the situation. In most cases, taking care of items in a timely manner for a resident may get you a great Google review, which can drive more traffic to the property. Resident retention is important; you do not want to have high turnover. Do all that you can to keep a resident happy. When a unit sits vacant, the owner loses money daily. This is what you must avoid, as owners do not like to lose money.

Advertising is important to keep units rented. With all the internet offers, this makes it easy for prospects to find properties all over the world. Apartment.com and Apartmentguide.com are great companies to assist with advertising. They also offer great packages for when your properties need help with vacancy. These are all important factors in the world of property management.

Managers understand what is expected of them by the owners. This is a huge investment for anyone that decides to purchase. They understand the return of their investment and want to make sure they have all pieces to generate the income they expect to make. So having a full idea of what comes next is important to have all the key factors to make it all come together so the property can be successful in the long term. Once you have the tools and understand all the components, you can thrive and move onto the property and continue the process. Property management is important and helps ease the owner's mind, knowing that they have full confidence of the team that they have placed to ensure the investment is protected and generates what they expect to collect monthly. Investors don't really get the opportunity to see how it all comes together. If the property makes money, everyone will make money. The circle of life, as we call it. Investors leave their trust in you to exceed all expectations that are presented. The team will make it all work for you, and you will be able to produce and show that they can place you in a position to manage other assets they require. Expand your horizon and show them your expertise: that you can grow the property to levels they have never seen before. Get a PROPERTY MANAGER!

Before you move forward reading this book, I want you to pause! Because after reading the do's and don'ts and all the info I just gave you, I'm sure fear has stepped in! This is the part where most people pull out and give up. The next chapter of this book will stop that from becoming your reality.

We added a chapter called "Transition," so that before you give up, maybe this chapter will give you a new perspective on how you see things, so that you will not talk yourself out of taking the first step to change, and motivative you to keep going no matter what. I'm sure for many this may have nothing to do with flipping houses. However, FEAR has a lot to do with everything. I read a lot of home books, and I didn't want this book to just be another real estate book. I realize we all need motivation sometimes, so here it is.

TRANSITION

Reality Check

Do you ever wonder why they call it the trap house? We hear about it all the time in music, but do you know what it's like to live in one? To have all your belongings piled up in the trunk of your car as you make your way to the area that was forbidden to visit. Pulling into the driveway to an all-brick duplex, looking at how lifeless the neighborhood appeared, and seeing the desperation in people's eyes on every corner. There was no love in this part of town. I arrived in Fifth Ward, the hood I would now call home. For months, I could hear roaches climbing in the walls while I slept on the couch. Waking up every day was a constant reminder that I had hit rock bottom. There was mold in the bathrooms, the water ran yellow for a while, the paint was peeling, the carpet smelled bad, and the wood was rotting. Every day I was confused, wondering how I got there. I was living in the trap house, and it was messing my head up. To the world, I had it all figured out. I was getting deals done, impacting people's lives, and being an asset to everyone's dreams. Yet, reality hit every time I pulled up into the driveway at the end of the night. I couldn't make *my* dreams come true.

I think it's safe to say that we've all gotten lost on our journey a time or two. Like you know what you should be doing, yet things seem to cloud your judgment, and give a false illusion of where you are and *who* you are. They call it the trap house because it's a mentality. The spirit of hopelessness was settling in, and I eventually felt like there was no way out. I was doing away with my responsibilities and avoiding the issue at hand. I was focusing more on how I got there, rather than asking *why* I was there. The teachings of Paulo Coelho were reminding me that "Every second of your search is an encounter with God." I was in the season of transition.

This season can be very traumatizing. It's a time of mental, emotional, and spiritual breakdowns. Fear, doubt, and depression rising over you; it's not the best feeling to have, nor the best place to be in. The key is to not give in to that feeling and allow those thoughts to consume your identity. When you feel those emotions coming over you, know that your higher self is requesting your undivided attention. Breaking barriers is not supposed to be easy. It's supposed to get dark when you're breaking generational curses. Sometimes you're called to the trenches to dig deep within to change the trajectory of your family's legacy. Times like these will determine what people will say about you in the history books. Sometimes you have to get uncomfortable to elevate. You have to do things you thought were beneath you, live in areas where you thought you would never call home, and go without to get the things you want. What are you willing to sacrifice for God to strengthen you? Sacrifice looks different to different people. For me, it was the time I was willing to spend in that brick house to make me who I am today.

Ego Death

I remember when I decided I wanted to skydive for my birthday. I was on edge and wanted to add a little bit of excitement to my life. All of my friends were hyping me up and wanted to join me. As the big day approached, phone calls stopped getting answered, and text messages responded with "Nah, I'm good." Until finally, it was just me. It was just me signing the paperwork, just me swiping my card, just me putting on my protective gear, just me walking towards the airplane. When I strapped into my seat, I realized my decision was final. Once those wheels came off the ground and into the air, my life flashed before my eyes. Everyone's opinions ran through my mind.

"What if you die?" they asked.

"I guess I'll go out with a bang...or splat," I replied jokingly. At that moment, my response was no longer funny.

I remember watching the pros sitting in front of me getting excited. Their adrenaline was amped up; they had been here before. The energy was high on the plane, and I had front-row seats to the drop-off. My heart pounded as I tried to get a glance to see the ground. Everything looked blurry, and the Earth looked like a big melting pot, with us in the sky stirring it up. When the first person jumped out of the plane, I thought they took my eyeballs with them. There was no turning back. It was at that moment I realized my life was about to change forever. The fear of not knowing how it was going to change had my anxiety high, my blood pumping, and my heart racing. I didn't know how things would end; I just knew I would never be the same. There was a thin line between the plane and the sky, and that thin line was me. I stood between me and my destiny; the choice to jump into the unknown yet knowing everything was going to be ok. I had to accept that I was here and know I was going to pull through this successfully on the other side. It was the same feeling I had in that trap house. You see, I want you to leverage that feeling, ride it for as long as you can, because that feeling is what's going to take you far. That feeling is going to help you make life-changing decisions. That feeling is what will set you apart and say enough is enough. If you find yourself having that feeling, this is the time to be radical, because you are now entering your journey of self-discovery.

Dare to be molded into the person you never knew you could become. Some people remain the same because they are afraid of the responsibility that comes with changing. They have a false illusion of thinking it's *real* to stay true to who you are and where you're from. They don't want to feel like a sell-out because we're taught it's an honor to live in the trenches. After jumping out of that plane on April 30, 2017, there was no way I could go home with the same mentality. I wasn't the same person; I couldn't be the same person. That day taught me *why*. That day revealed to me that fear was the only thing trapping me in my negative thoughts. On that day, all of my fears were released into the sky. I landed on the ground with a restored mind and sound thoughts. I knew then I could overcome anything. Shortly after, I started my new business, I began traveling for a living, and was meeting some of the most dynamic people I would've never met had I not put myself out there.

It's easy to get caught up in the darkness. We focus on where we want to be and forget that where we are is what we prayed for back then. Don't let that go over your head. Be grateful, give yourself credit, and find beauty in your process of evolution. You need that fear to challenge you. Lean into it and own it, because you can mold that fear into whatever you want it to become. That fear will give birth to your desired results. Those results can end in defeat or victory.

Process Then Become

You are living in the prayers you said five years ago. However, the trials of today are distracting you from feeling a sense of deliverance and accomplishments. Try to recall what you asked God to help you with years ago, then ask yourself: was it done? Understand that it takes time, focus, and determination to open the doors to infinity.

I remember moving into my new place and staring at all the rooms with white walls. I had the choice to decide how I wanted each room to look. I could keep them all white, add some decorations, paint the walls, or I could even write on them. Once I decided how I wanted the walls to look, then the real work began. I had to put the time into researching where I was going to find all the materials, the paint, and the fabrics to add texture to my new home. It was the same approach I had to take in deciding how I wanted my life to look. I had to hold that image in my head and do the research to learn what it takes to become the person who lives a life. Then, I had to add those textures into my life. I had to change the way I dressed, read more books, further my education, go to more networking events, and become more business savvy. I had to challenge myself and do what was necessary to possess the qualities that would enhance my lifestyle.

Regardless of how you want this finished version of yourself to look, you have to put the time in to understanding the tools you are going to need. Once those tools start arriving, get excited. Most of the time, when we start getting the tools, we get depressed because we think about how much work it's going to be. We start seeing the tools we asked for from a negative standpoint, like, "*Ugh this is going to add more stress.*" It's common to think this because our mind is naturally in overdrive, and it seems like you can never catch a break. However, this is a time to be positive and get excited *because* your tools came in, which means your life is getting ready to transform. You shouldn't see transitioning as a burden, it's a reason to be grateful, because you need those tools to enhance your way of thinking and your quality of life. You need those tools to work your muscles, to expand your mind, to push you to the limits, to get you one step closer to the finished masterpiece. It's the same thing with the walls in every room; you're transforming it into what you want it to become.

Once you receive your tools, it's now time to put them to work. If you don't want to get lost in the sauce, there's a process you must follow to ensure the tools work in your favor.

Some people may get their tools all at once, while others may get a few now and the rest later. Regardless, where people go wrong is trying to use the tools all at once. You're testing them out versus using them how they were fully designed to function one at a time. It's the same thing with those rooms. Everything gets delivered to the house, and you're trying to hang up all the photos, install all the lights, and move in all the furniture. If you try to do everything at once, you risk getting frustrated if it doesn't come together the way you want it to, or worse, you break something because you were rushing the process. Don't overwhelm yourself trying to do the most. Time is of the essence, and you have to adjust one thing at a time, just as you would with your life. Give yourself time to learn each of your tools. Build a psychological relationship with your tools, and allow your brain to understand how to use the tools in their best form. Let the tools become a part of your character and become second nature to you. Don't get caught up in trying to skim through the process. You'll burn yourself out trying to overload your mind, then only gain temporary satisfaction from things you've been waiting for to add value to your life. No matter how bad you want those rooms done and your life different, it can't get done any faster than its due date. You can't skip steps, so find joy in *becoming* during your transition. Give yourself time to go through the stages of metamorphosis and to mature all of your emotions.

Forever Evolving

I remember watching a video of this reporter who asked Bill Gates, "What did it take to become successful?" He pulled out a blank check and told her to write any amount she wanted on the check. Surprised by the gesture, she immediately said no. He told her again to write any amount on the check she wanted, and again she respectfully declined. He insisted one last time to write any amount on the check, and her final response was no. To answer her question, he told her that *the reason he became successful was because he maximized every opportunity presented to him.*

We've been raised off many cliches, one of which is "Some things are too good to be true." Why is that? Why have we groomed ourselves to think there's a catch to everything, or that we are not worthy of an opportunity that is needed? A lot of people remain the same because they let their pride hold them down like an anchor. Just like that reporter, many of us have been placed in a position to change the legacy of our family and be given direct access to generational wealth. Yet, we let these opportunities slip between our fingers. The truth is it takes a certain individual to recognize what has to be done in order to achieve this. There's a certain level of intelligence and focus needed to identify the areas that need constant reinvention. This will help you climb higher heights, go the distance, and obtain the success you desire.

It's the same thing with living in the trap house. I had to realize that I wasn't trapped, I was just misunderstanding the bricks around me. I was hiding behind the brick walls to mask my pain, disparity, and brokenness. There was a process I had to undergo to break the barriers of those bricks, then realign the structure of my foundation. Once I began to see the house differently, I was able to imagine my situation differently. That experience showed me what I was made of even when it appeared like there was no way out. I needed that season in my life to help me understand what elements to strengthen from within. And for that, I appreciate the time it took to cultivate this new being because it taught me the art of flipping bricks.

– Berry Dynamic @ McNair Books

ENDURANCE

I'm Tiffany Veney, born and raised in the inner city of East Baltimore. My background is typical of any inner-city child in the '80s. My mother was addicted to drugs, my father was in prison, and I was raised by my grandmother. Since I was the oldest of seven kids, I was tasked with taking care of my siblings. I hated it lol. I grew up with the two eldest. Two of them were adopted, one was raised by an extended family member, and the baby was raised primarily by his dad. Although my grandmother raised me, I was still in foster care. Despite the struggle, I wouldn't change anything. I wouldn't be as resilient today without going through all the challenges I've endured.

The only thing I feel sets me apart is that I always believed there was more out there for me. I'm blessed to still have been shown a different way out. Whether it was going to the house of the people I worked for (at age twelve—yes, before a work permit), who lived in Essex off the water, or being in the Living Classroom Program. I've always been determined to not let my situation define me.

As a child, I was always intrigued by home renovations. In fact, I really wanted to be a construction worker. I quickly erased that from my mind, though, because I told myself that it was a manly job. I later begged to go to Baltimore Polytechnic Institute, because I felt like engineering was the next best thing. In college, I studied architecture then quickly switched my major to Finance. I convinced myself, mainly due to the lack of women in the industry, that I needed to go with a safer field.

At 25, I bought my first house. I felt so accomplished and ahead of the game. I made some bad financial decisions and lost it a few years later. I still think Wells Fargo owes me for that due to their unsavory loan modification processes back then, but I digress. I still learned a lot from that situation, and one of the most important lessons was the importance of home ownership. Home ownership is a great accomplishment. It can create generational wealth, it becomes an asset you can later leverage, and it also gives a great sense of pride in your neighborhood. I now look at real estate as a tool to financial freedom. Whether it's the property you occupy or one you rent out, there's several opportunities to make money from real estate. The caveat is that there's also tons of ways to lose in real estate as well. Before making a purchase, you should look at the current value of homes, their current condition, the cost to bring the home up to date if needed, and if the asking price falls within or under the market price.

I decided to get my real estate license when I was 25, but unfortunately that was right when the housing market crashed, so I stayed in finance. Years later, I tried property management, and that was more hands on, but not in the right direction. After working for someone else managing their rehab projects for a few years, I decided to start my own business and take on my own projects. I'm still amazed by the transformations that can take place. Whether it's residential or commercial, I view it as a blank canvas with endless opportunities. I love to be innovative, creative, functional and modern. So remember, if I can do it, you can too!

– Tiffany Veney, CEO Madison Street Designs

RESOURCES

Virgil Gordon II is the CEO of Power Purchase Mortgage, one of the most successful self-sustained multi-million-dollar mortgage companies in Atlanta, GA. Although the company's headquarters is located in the state of GA, Virgil is still able to originate loans in other states such as Florida and Tennessee. Virgil has served as an idol and a blessing to many for his diligence and dedication to obtaining satisfactory results for his clients. He has easily been identified as one of the most reliable go-to lenders who specializes in the execution of multi-million-dollar loans.

The company has generated well over 100 million in revenue within the past year alone. He regularly services opulent accounts, which have included affluent business owners, athletes, and celebrities. His company is most recognized for his personalized approach to producing funding opportunities for entrepreneurial clients using a program known as the Entrepreneur Bank Statement Loan. The program's popularity stems from allowing clients an opportunity to obtain funding without the use of tax returns.

This program is a big hit with applicants who own at least 50%–100% of their company, have been self-employed for two or more years, have a minimum FICO of 660, and are able to make a down payment of 10%–15% on a 30 year fixed rate mortgage. Power Purchase Mortgage will consider applicants with DTI of up to 50%. Applicants looking for better terms on their current home mortgage are able to benefit greatly through Power Purchase Mortgage by applying for the cash-out refinance program, which can cover up to 85% LTV. The only documentation needed to qualify is a copy of the applicant's driver's license, social security number, and 12 months of business bank statements.

In addition to the aforementioned programs, Power Purchase Mortgage also has flexible qualification guidelines through their Minimal Doc loan program. The Minimal Doc program allows applicants the option to provide either 12 months of personal bank statements or business bank statements and can issue funding for a primary, investment, second home purchase or refinance, with interest rates of between 4.250% and 6.50%. Applicants looking for funding for short sales, foreclosures, bankruptcy, or deed-in lieu projects must have a minimum two years of experience.

As with most loans, the better the credit score, the better the terms. Applicants with a credit score of 700+ qualify for the 10% down payment, while applicants with a credit score of 660–699 will require 15%. Loans can be funded up to $4 million. If you are ready to invest in your future with real estate with one of the best companies around, be sure to visit www.powerpurchasemortgage.com and apply today.

NOTES

_____

_____

_____

_____

_____

_____

_____

_____

_____

_____

_____

NOTES

_____

_____

_____

_____

_____

_____

_____

_____

_____

_____

_____

_____

NOTES

_____

_____

_____

_____

_____

_____

_____

_____

_____

_____

_____

NOTES

_____

_____

_____

_____

_____

_____

_____

_____

_____

_____

_____

NOTES

_____

_____

_____

_____

_____

_____

_____

_____

_____

_____

_____

NOTES

_____

_____

_____

_____

_____

_____

_____

_____

_____

_____

_____

_____

NOTES

NOTES

_____

_____

_____

_____

_____

_____

_____

_____

_____

_____

_____

NOTES

_____

_____

_____

_____

_____

_____

_____

_____

_____

_____

NOTES

_____

_____

_____

_____

_____

_____

_____

_____

_____

_____

_____

NOTES

NOTES

_____

_____

_____

_____

_____

_____

_____

_____

_____

_____

_____

NOTES

NOTES

_____

_____

_____

_____

_____

_____

_____

_____

_____

_____

_____

NOTES

_____

_____

_____

_____

_____

_____

_____

_____

_____

_____

NOTES

_____

_____

_____

_____

_____

_____

_____

_____

_____

_____

_____

_____

NOTES

_____

_____

_____

_____

_____

_____

_____

_____

_____

_____

_____

_____

NOTES

_____

_____

_____

_____

_____

_____

_____

_____

_____

_____

_____

NOTES

_____

_____

_____

_____

_____

_____

_____

_____

_____

_____

_____

NOTES

_____

_____

_____

_____

_____

_____

_____

_____

_____

_____

_____

_____

NOTES

NOTES

_____

_____

_____

_____

_____

_____

_____

_____

_____

_____

_____

_____

NOTES

_____

_____

_____

_____

_____

_____

_____

_____

_____

_____

_____

NOTES

DOUGLAS PARSON JR.

NOTES

_____

_____

_____

_____

_____

_____

_____

_____

_____

_____

_____

NOTES

_____

_____

_____

_____

_____

_____

_____

_____

_____

_____

_____

NOTES

www.ingramcontent.com/pod-product-compliance
Lightning Source LLC
Chambersburg PA
CBHW062100270326
41931CB00013B/3154